Around Cannock Cl....

on old picture postcards

Eric Woolley

Cannock.

1. A rather deserted view of Cannock Market Place about 1912, looking towards the bowling green – and not a motor vehicle in sight. The shop on the extreme right was Wooton's. Postcard published at the *Advertiser* office, Cannock.

£3.50

**Designed and Published by
Reflections of a Bygone Age,
Keyworth, Nottingham
1995**

ISBN 0 946245 92 4

**Printed by
Adlard Print and Typesetting Services,
Ruddington, Notts.**

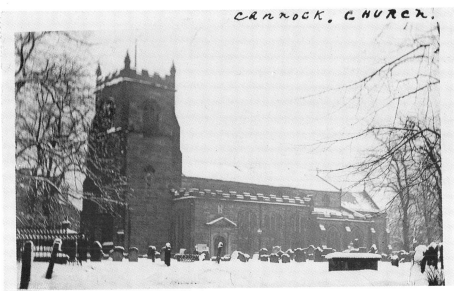

2. The church of St. Luke, Cannock, is a stone edifice consisting of a chancel, clerestoried nave of six bays, aisles and an embattled tower with a clock and six bells. Cannock was referred to as a parish church by the Bishop of Coventry and Lichfield as far back as 1293, and a treasured possession is an oak chest, said to be 14th century. This photograph shows the church during the winter of 1909; the card was posted to the vicarage at Hall Green, Birmingham in March 1909.

3. The Urban District Council Offices were in Church Street before new premises were acquired in High Green in 1926 and opened the following year. This card, published by a local printer called V.L. Withington, was posted to Wolverhampton in September 1913. Withington was the proprietor of the *Cannock Advertiser.*

INTRODUCTION

Cannock, Hednesford, Rugeley and other towns and villages represented on old picture postcards in this book all sprang up around "The Chase", which itself covers 3000 acres of land which past monarchs once used for hunting grounds. "The Chase" was a desolate area, where it has been said that wolves prowled, and outlaws and vagabonds sought refuge. The towns prospered and became extended when the coal industry came to life, and during the Great War of 1914-18 Cannock Chase was used for billeting Commonwealth forces from Australia and New Zealand as well as British battalions. Rare views such as the "Tackeroo express" and a later card showing several Bevan boys are included in the book which gives an insight to the days when the picture postcard was a very popular medium of correspondence and seven mail deliveries a day was common practice within the postal system. Photographic view cards by small local publishers are well represented and are sure to create many talking points around the area.

1994 saw the centenary of the British picture postcard, and an upsurge in this field of collecting has seen the hobby grow immensely to become almost as popular as stamps.

Eric Woolley
January 1995

I am extremely grateful to Nigel Bailey for his help and the loan of his postcard collection. Many of Nigel's cards are included in this publication.

Back cover (top): five pictures of Rugeley on one card. Featured are Brook Street, The Chase, Horn's Pool, Upper Brook Street and a view of soldiers. The postcard was published by W. Shaw of Burslem about 1912.

    (bottom): a view of High Street, Chasetown, with the "Junction Inn" on the right. Chasetown is on Cannock Chase, and was a mining community, with most of the workers employed at the extensive collieries first opened in 1849 by the Marquis of Anglesey and later taken over by the Cannock Chase Colliery Co. Ltd. Card published by G. Lawson of Chasetown and posted at Selly Oak in August 1910.

OUR GLORIOUS DEAD

4. The war memorial situated in the square was erected in 1923 at a cost of £600, to the memory of the men from the town who gave their lives during the 1914-18 war. Built on a granite base, it depicts a soldier and a sailor from that conflict.

5. One of the better photographic postcards of the area is this 1913 view of Church Street, Cannock, from the camera of A.W. Mills, who operated from Lichfield. Note the two young lads with the old pram in the centre left of the scene, which is typical of this period. The card was posted from Cannock in March 1913 and sent to Kensington.

(MILLS PHOTO Nº3901)

Market Place, Cannock.

6. Cannock Market Place, with most of the shops recognisable by name. The *Cannock Advertiser's* premises are prominent behind the signpost, while to the left of the photo are The People's coffee house, tobacconist E.L. Keight, and Hunter's tea stores. A lone cyclist is the only traffic in sight, a great contrast to today's Cannock.

MARKET PLACE, CANNOCK.

G.4706.

7. A 1930s view of Cannock Market Place looking towards Wolverhampton Road. The motor car passing Foster Bros.is turning towards High Green and Penkridge Road. The Maypole Dairy Co. and Taylor's chemists are to the left of the picture. The postcard was sent to Bath in August 1937.

8. A lovely photographic card of the "Hippodrome" theatre (later to become the "Forum" picture house) in Cannock Market Place. A dozen or so people have posed for the camera at the entrance to the circle, including a gentleman – probably the manager – wearing a large top hat. The card appears to be from the 1915-20 period.

9. The "Royal Oak Inn" in the Market Place on a 1906 card. Licensee at the time was Robert Grigg – possibly the man posing by the entrance. The postcard was sent to Miss Taylor at the refreshment rooms on Birmingham New Street railway station in March 1906.

10. Another card of Market Square, Cannock, featuring an unfamiliar view in the days before World War One. Hewson's shop is on the left.

11. This card of High Green dates from the late 1930s with the trees in full bloom. It was here that the New Hall was built in 1892 by F.D. Bumsted. A structure of red brick with stone dressings, the hall had a large room, big enough to seat 500 people. It was used by the church for Sunday School meetings, lectures, and concerts.

12. A huge crowd gathered to witness the proclamation of King George V in Cannock Market Place. A.H. Swift's grocer's shop is on the right.

Bandstand & Bowling Green, Cannock

Published at "The Advertiser" Office, Cannock

13. This 1906 card of the bowling green also shows the bandstand in front of the large lime trees. This pleasant spot was supported and maintained entirely by subscriptions from local people. A trust was formed in October 1896 to look after the "Green" and to preserve the grounds forever to be used as a bowling green. This terminated on 31st December 1935. Another card published by the *Advertiser,* and posted in October 1906.

CRICKET GROUND CANNOCK PARK

14. A photographic card by Withington of the cricket ground in Cannock Park, with a game in progress. The card was posted to Carlisle in September 1937.

15. A postcard of the "Crown" Hotel published in 1914 by the *Advertiser*. According to the caption, this is how the building appeared "in olden times".

16. Queen's Hall during the late 1930s. This building on Allport Road was a dance hall managed by Arthur Ernest Thomas before the Second World War, and later became the premises of the Swallow raincoat company. Card published in 'Praill's Series' and posted at Hednesford in August 1942.

17. The staff of the National Provincial Bank outside the entrance to their building, which stood in High Green. The card was published by local photographer Fred Parsons.

18. Members of the Sunday School teaching staff of the Cannock Parish Church – and the vicar – on a festival day c.1910.

19. The church at Bridgtown was erected in 1899. The mission of St. Paul cost £2,000 and was built of red brick to seat 350 members of the congregation. It replaced an older building. Photographic card by unidentified publisher.

20. An unusual picture of an impromptu jazz band at Bridgtown enjoying the peace celebrations after World War One.

21. This traction engine and trailer was the property of the Cannock Agricultural Co. Ltd., and was built by the firm of Ransomes. The CA Co. was based at Bridgtown and were manufacturers of chemical bone manure and also implement makers and seedsmen. They had another depot at Churchbridge railway goods yard.

22. An early postcard, mailed in July 1904, showing the hospital at Cheslyn Hay which was used for isolating patients suffering from contagious diseases. The Cannock rural council built the hospital in 1904 at a cost of almost £2,000; it could accommodate twenty patients.

CHESLYN HAY.

23. A lovely old photographic postcard of the United Methodist Church at Cheslyn Hay, built in 1855 and enlarged in 1898 to seat a congregation of 600. A new organ was installed at a cost of £500. This card was posted to Edgbaston in June 1908.

24. *"How do you like this, it is the band going to the flower s*
ton in August 1909. The procession is passing the "Crowr
lished card.

"went the message on this card posted to Wolverhamp-
and Sellman's shop. A superb, but anonymously-pub-

25. The war memorial at Cheslyn Hay is situated at the top of Station Street near the junction of High and Low Streets. It was unveiled in front of a large crowd of people from the parish on August 14th 1921. Both these cards were published by a local firm called Snape from nearby Bridgtown. On the one above, the drapes are still in place, and the congregation has heads bowed observing a minute's silence.

26. The unveiled memorial, with the inscriptions showing the names of the gallant men from the parish who lost their lives during the Great War.

Hilton Hall.

27. Hilton Hall was the seat of Walter B.W. Vernon J.P. An old mansion, built in red brick with stone dressings, it was altered and extended in 1830. The hall had around 100 acres of land, on which a tower was erected in 1741 to commemorate the taking of Porto Bello by Admiral Vernon in November 1739. The card was posted at Cheslyn Hay in February 1905.

Shoal Hill, Cannock.

28. Many postcards of Shoal Hill exist, as this beauty spot on the Chase was very popular with local children, as can be seen on this 1912 card published by the *Advertiser.*

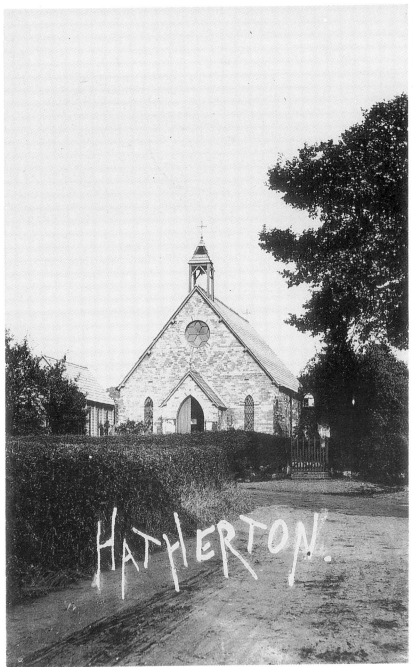

HATHERTON.

29. There are few postcards around of Hatherton, so this fine photographic example of the church is a very rare find. The Church of St. Thomas was built in 1872 by Edward Richard, who was then 2nd Baron Hatherton C.B. It was enlarged in 1879 to hold about 140 people.

INFANTS' AND GIRLS' SCHOOL, CHADSMOOR

30. The infants' and girls' school at Chadsmoor about 1920 on a 'Praill's Series' postcard.

INTERIOR ST. CHADS. CHADSMOOR.

31. The interior of St. Chad's Church at Chadsmoor, built in 1891, at a cost of £2,600, in Gothic style of red brick. The church has a chancel, nave, South porch and organ chamber, and a western turret with one bell. In 1924 a rood and screen was erected to the memory of 60 men from Chadsmoor who died in the First World War.

32. An excellent animated scene of Market Street, Hednesford dominated by the London & North Western Railway bus approaching the cameraman. On the corner of Market Street is Rhodes' fancy goods and toy warehouse while Ellis's sweet shop is on the right. The card was published by Rhodes and posted to Birmingham in August 1918.

33. An interesting study of E. Webb's jeweller's shop in Market Street. He also specialised in watches and spectacles. Card posted at Hednesford in May 1916.

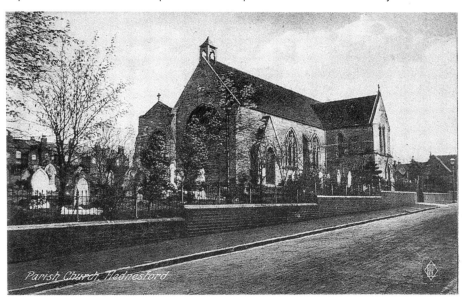

34. The parish church of St. Luke, Hednesford, underwent repairs and improvements in 1882 at a cost of £2,802. A new organ was installed in 1914, costing £1,000. It houses a congregation of 900.

MARKET STREET, HEDNESFORD. *Goscombe Photo.*

35. Attractive card of Hednesford's Market Street published by Goscombe, a little-known firm in the postcard field. Note the lighting above the shop on the extreme left of the card, and the barber's pole next door.

View of Hednesford from Church Hill.

36. Looking down Church Hill, Hednesford, with the Chase in the background, and earthworks on the left. Card published by J. Bird, hairdresser, Hednesford.

37. An unusual card from about 1905. Stafford Lane is featured on the top picture and the waterworks below the caption. These works on Rugeley Road supplied most of the town's water supply and were owned by the South Staffordshire Water Works Co.

38. This card provides views of some of the important collieries on Cannock Chase: Littleton, Leacroft, Old Coppice and East Cannock. The card was sent to Gateshead in September 1916.

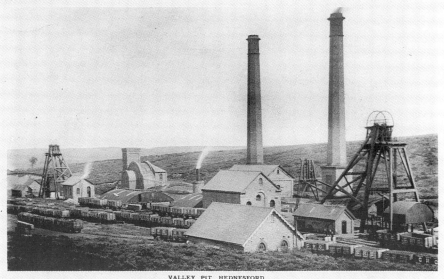

VALLEY PIT, HEDNESFORD.

39. Valley pit at Hednesford was just one of several coal mines in the area worked by the Cannock and Rugeley Colliery Co. Ltd., The Cannock Chase Colliery Co. Ltd., and The East Cannock and West Cannock Co. Ltd. Each had extensive works in the area. Views of the pithead and winding gear are clearly visible on this postcard published by the local firm of Rhodes. It was sent to Liverpool in December 1911.

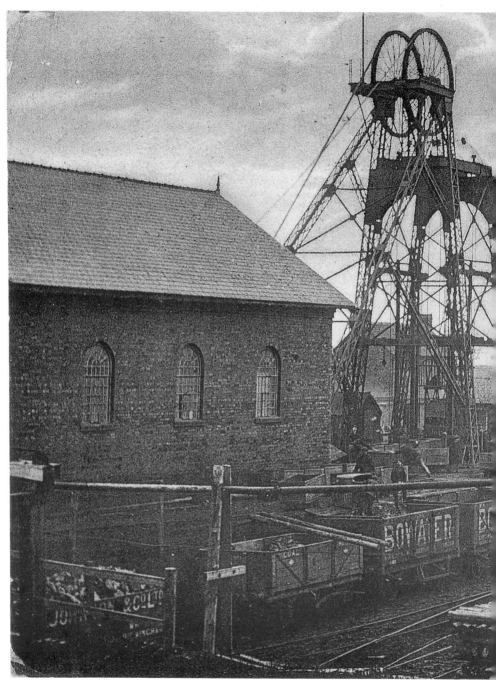

40. Close-up of the pithead and winding gear at Leacroft Colliery. Leacroft was a small community and hamlet one mile south-east of Cannock at the time the card was published by the *Cannock Advertiser* in 1913.

Leacroft Colliery, Cannock.

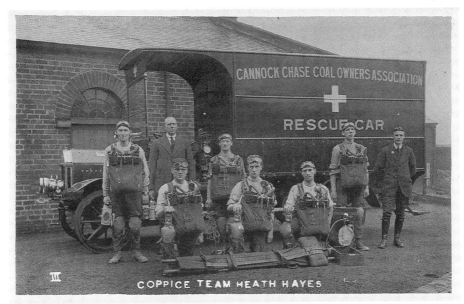

41. The Cannock Chase Coal Owners Association provided their rescue teams with motor vehicles like the one illustrated here. The Heath Hayes team pose here fully equipped to deal with emergencies whenever they happened. Card published by G. Stacey of Hednesford.

42. A group of 'Bevan' boys – named after politician Aneurin Bevan – who were conscripted during the Second World War to work in the pits instead of joining the armed forces. These lads are standing in front of the miners' hostel at Wimblebury in 1944.

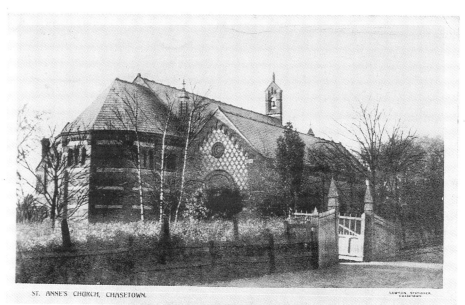

ST. ANNE'S CHURCH, CHASETOWN.

43. The church of St. Anne's at Chasetown was built entirely from the funds of J.R. McLean Esq., and was brick-built with Bath stone dressings in the Romanesque style. The church register dates from 1867, and the interior could accommodate 700 worshippers. The card was published by Lawton of Chasetown.

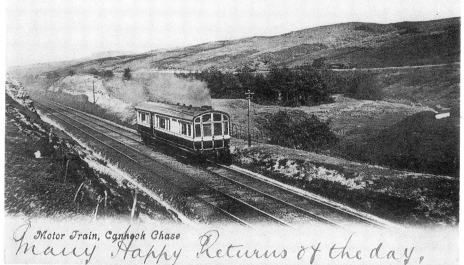

Motor Train, Cannock Chase

many Happy Returns of the day,

44. The Chase is to the east of Cannock and covers around 30,000 acres of land containing a good light soil. Turnips and corn were grown and it was also a suitable area for pasture. During the Great War, army camps were set up on the Chase with men from Commonwealth countries such as New Zealand billeted there, along with many British infantry regiments. This card by De Vall of Rugeley shows an L.N.W.R. motor train crossing the Chase, travelling between Hednesford and Rugeley about 1910.

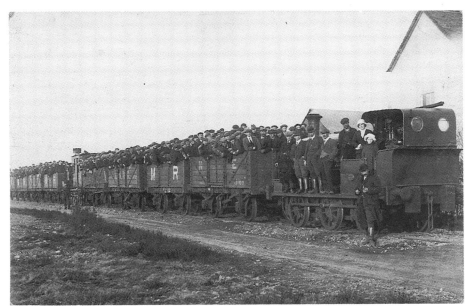

45. The small locomotive that carried workers across the Chase to various sites between Cannock and Rugeley was affectionately known as the "Tackeroo Express" – it even had a song written in its honour and featured on the reverse of this postcard by Alfred Bates of Rugeley.

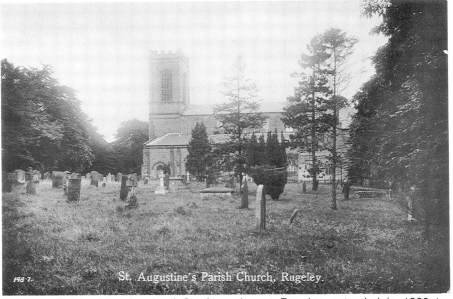

St. Augustine's Parish Church, Rugeley.

46. The Gothic-style church of St. Augustine at Rugeley, extended in 1906 to accommodate a congregation of 700. Card by Wood of Rugeley.

The Horse Fair, Rugeley.

47. A fine picture of the Horse Fair at Rugeley. Fairs were held each year for six days beginning on June 1st. Colts and horses *'of a superior description'* (according to one journalist) were sold, and stock sales held every other Tuesday. In this Edwardian card published by Pascoe & Son of Rugeley, the "Globe" Hotel can be seen in the centre distance.

Church Street, Rugeley.

48. Church Street, Rugeley on a c.1902 postcard, deserted of traffic but with several children visible. Six cottages in the street were built by the Misses Sneyd in 1836, along with others erected in1870 by the direction of H.R.Sneyd for *"poor old women"*.

THE SPOT WHERE THE LIVING HORSE WAS FOUND GRAZING.

BROOMHILL FARM, WHERE THE OUTRAGE WAS COMMITTED.

WHERE THE ENTRAILS OF THE DEAD HORSE WERE FOUND.

THE CATTLE MAIMING OUTRAGES AT GREAT WYRLEY.

GT WYRLEY PARISH CHURCH.

THE CORNER OF THE FIELD WHERE THE DEAD HORSE WAS FOUND.

49. On the morning of 1st February 1903, a horse was found cruelly slaughtered at Great Wyrley. It proved to be the first of a series of similar crimes, depicted on this postcard detailing "the cattle maiming outrages" published by the Birmingham firm of Scott Russell & Co. A local solicitor, son of the vicar of Great Wyrley, was arrested, convicted of the atrocities and given a seven-year prison sentence. After a public protest, George Edolji was given a king's pardon after the verdict proved to be a miscarriage of justice. No-one else was ever arrested for the crimes.

SISTERS' QUARTERS. M of P HOSPITAL, CANNOCK CHASE

50. The military hospital on Cannock Chase featured during severe winter conditions c.1920 on a card in the 'Park' series.